Aligning

Partnering with Soul

Poems

By

Deborah Draves Legg

2021 Copyright © Deborah Draves Legg

All rights reserved. No part of the publication may be reproduced or transmitted in any form or by any means, electronic or mechanical, including photocopying, recording or by an information storage and retrieval system without permission in writing from the author. Reviewers may quote short passages.
ISBN: 978-1-7378773-0-1

Designed and written by Deborah Draves Legg
Photography: Sandy Sharkey, Deborah Draves Legg and Sissel Nystad

First edition published 2021
Contact: Deborah Draves Legg
www.eponicity.com

Dedication

To my partner, my soul.

Table Of Contents

Preface...5
The King's Gambit...8
The Cosmic Contract...10
Processing 2020...11
Wizard, Warrior and Wonder...15
Resilience...18
Mission Possible...20
Journey of a Soul Family...22
White Bones...24
Warning: Colony Collapse...26
Honoring My Twin...28
Remembering Beauty...29
The Dual Pilgrimage - Ode to Juano...33
My Steve...36
Rise Up or Up Rise...38
The Great Turning Over...40
Pollinators...42
Hot Air Balloon...44
Re-Wilding...46
An Ode to Wild Souls...48
Pillars of Grief...50
Mime to Have Some Fun...52
The Choice...54
Passings...56
Trinity...58
Faith in Unfurling...60
Soul Parenting...62
Game On...64

Preface

The day I knew there was more to the world than meets the eye.

On this day, sometime in 2012, I was working with a family in a small clearing at our (former) retreat center in Costa Rica; Dorado was my equine co-facilitator. It was our third day together, exploring the way family dynamics naturally correlate to herd dynamics. On the previous days, as well as on this day, a large bee was bugging us. It was a tropical species that lives in small colonies consisting of about ten members. They are huge, the size of a ping pong ball; their ambling flight is clumsy and appears directionless. By this, the third day, the bee was buzzing around us again; I shooed it away, but it just came back. I decided I was going to have to kill it. Although they are not aggressive when they do sting, it is excruciating; I didn't want anyone to get stung.

The 5 of us were standing in a circle, me, the family of 3, and Dorado, who was at liberty (not tied up) in the small open arena. I aimed to swat the bee down to the ground and step on it, but just as I raised my hand, Dorado stepped in between me and the bee and 'grabbed' the bee with his forehead. He proceeded to bounce the bee on his forehead while he trotted to the edge of the clearing. With a toss of his head, he slung the bee into the rainforest, then trotted back to our circle. We all looked at each other, wide-eyed, and wondered if we really saw what we just saw.

Dorado was standing directly in front of me, staring at me. I thanked him for saving us from the bee, but he didn't budge; his steady gaze pierced right through me. Then I realized he had not saved us from the bee; he saved the bee from me. Upon this realization, Dorado relaxed and started eating grass...message received.

Wow, that day, I experienced a connection to an unseen, benevolently connected world, despite human indifference.

During my time in Costa Rica, hundreds of clients passed in to and out of the magical world of unseen but profoundly felt connection. They reconnected to themselves, others, and nature, forever changed by their experiences supported by horses in the rain forest, as was I.

This new way of being in the world prepared me for one of the most evolutionary times of my life. In 2019 we decided to sell our retreat center and create a new project in Costa Rica. We sold the hotel in late 2019; however, for an unknown reason, the deal fell through, leaving us perplexed. What did the universe want from us or want for us?

I needed some time away to contemplate. In February 2020, I flew to Miami to visit a friend. When the time came for me to go back to Costa Rica, I was not ready. I extended my stay and headed to Charlottesville, VA, to visit another friend. I drove north from Miami on Interstate 75. When passing the exits for Sarasota, two meaningful songs came on the radio that we played at our wedding. Suddenly, it hit me; we were meant to move back to the USA. The date was February 14th, 2020, exactly 14 years since my husband, Steve, and I were driving south from Sarasota to Miami to begin our adventure in Costa Rica. Two seven-year cycles had been completed. I cried all the way to Virginia.

I returned to Costa Rica the last week of February 2020 to a hotel full of guests. The threat of the pandemic was rising from background noise into the foreground. The Costa Rican government wanted all tourists out of the country; the airlines began contacting our guests to repatriate them back to their home countries. On March 19th, all the airports were closing, and we had to make the most difficult decision of our lives: to stay or go back to the USA. There would be no tourism for an unknown amount of time, and I could work as a nurse in the USA until we could reopen. We felt we had to go back to be with our family and elderly parents; the virus' wrath was uncertain. Saying goodbye to the world that we loved, not knowing if we'd ever see anyone again, was the hardest thing I've ever had to do in my life.

In April 2020, the day I was to sign a travel nurse contract, the same buyer for the hotel made another offer. We took it, and the deal went through. During the following months, I started to align with my Soul in a new way, the next way. The lockdown was my cocoon. I spent the time transforming what no longer served me into the wisdom that would support me going forward. These are the poems of Soul during that time of transformation.

The photographs in this collection are of my horses in Costa Rica and Virginia.

The King's Gambit

Twin star seeds planted in tandem
A soul contract, their connection was anything but random
However; remember, the cosmos offers free choice
Stay silent and hide, or trust, be brave and be the voice

Twin number one, her good seed planted on Earth
Twin number two, his good seed spent his time on Earth
Together they were, sometimes in form, but always in spirit
Their years together as human and horse seemed like only a minute

A pandemic blew in and dumped them into quicksand
She had to leave him in haste and go back to her native land
A time so confusing, so many decisions to make, just to be safe
Goodbye was the only choice she could make

Weeping in the rain, she fell to her knees, at his loyal feet
"I cannot leave you; what will I do? Oh, why did we meet?"
He assured her, "We've planted our seeds; a good forest is growing."
She cried, "All along, I believed our work, here, was the grand knowing."

She pulled herself up, his soft breath whispered, "Dear, do not grieve."
Using his royal head, he pushed her out of the pasture,
"Go now, my dear, it's time to leave."
"It was I that sent your man to protect you; he is our knight."
"He is me as I am him; we will protect you both day and night."

She felt weak and defeated, tears flowing laden with pain
"Trust and be brave, I will join you when it is time to begin our next reign."
"You must go now," he said, "It is time."
"My dear, you will be fine, and will always be mine."

The Cosmic Contract

Soul says,
    Hear me Ego
    Listen to me and away we go
    The world is not as it seems
    Imagine it, see it, live your dreams
Ego says,
    Is that really you Soul?
    Guide me to reach our goal
    Show me what is possible
    To believe that nothing is impossible
Soul says,
    Remember I steer the ship
    When I've got your back, we'll go at a pretty fast clip
    By embracing your transformations
    You'll have unlimited manifestations
Ego says,
    I will crew our ship
    Send me the orders, I'll give you no lip
    I welcome your love to fuel my transformations
    And fully embrace all of your manifestations

Processing 2020

My grief stands alone
In the shadows where the sun once shown
All that was left behind
Created in love and one of a kind

A tiny town, our community
We were taken in, they thought we built in futility
A strange land, it was an adventure in any case
Fueled by an unknown force, some would call faith

We dreamed it, we planned it
Built it, expanded it; there wasn't much time to sit
People came from near and far
Many came just to drink a Shrek at the Lava Lizard Bar

Suddenly, the world, our world was shaken
A pandemic, an ominous veil, all was forsaken
Confronted with a choice, but how could we choose?
Leaving this place, there was so much to lose

Our family in the USA, our roots
A strong knowing, existed in the unknown, shocked and mute
The virus forced our hand, we had no voice
Discussing the options, in the end, we had no choice

Leaving our life, our dream, our friends… Humans, horses, our land, is it possible that we will ever mend?
To leave, to lose all that we created
Has severed a part of me that may never heal, forever deflated

What is the meaning, the reason?
It's all too much for this human being
Some of my horses have died
Denied the chance to be by their side

What is the meaning, the reason?
At first all I felt like doing was screaming
Tears where unstoppable
Getting over it seemed so impossible

Looking back on the years
Many ups and downs, times filled with fears
Two cycles of seven
Experiences sent down from heaven

To make sense of it all to be certain it's over
I must appreciate the luck like a four leaf clover
Processing the stories, adventures, comradery
Looking back at it all, feels like one long odyssey!

The experience was how to create community
The emotion was joy, love and loyalty
The experience is learning to let go
The emotion is sadness and grief, let the tears flow

The experience is that I am protected
The meaning is that everything is connected
The action is to take, honor this new space
The next transformation will come, in this I have faith

Wizard, Warrior and Wonder

My beloved, good Wizard, Dorado, whom a pointed cap would not fit
It was not your physical existence that sparked an eternal fire that you lit
In our 12 years together, you showed me a new world full of wonder
A warrior of fairness and love, your power to heal was your thunder

Your time before we met, speed and agility brought you to fame
Around the barrels you ran, rodeo fans loudly cheered out your name
When the old life was complete, it was our time to gather together
Our souls had prepared us to work together like wings of a feather

Your golden mane has been held by many tight knuckles
The thought of riding a horse makes many knees buckle
In incredible circumstances, you remained calm and stoic
A Warrior valiant and loyal, the definition of heroic

You showed connection without judgment, authentic relationship
A light being, cloaked as a horse, maybe you came from some spaceship
Time after time, you taught what it meant to be honest and true
It is how humans claim that they live; however, most don't have a clue

One day as we worked with a family outside
A giant bee buzzed around us; it was an incredible size
With intention to protect the small child from a sting
I aimed at the bee, swung at him, I intended to kill him, you see

You halted my swing, stepping right in my path
Bounced the bee on your forehead, protecting us from its wrath
You trotted away with the bee on your head to the edge of the forest
The bee then flew off, joining the other insects all a buzz in a chorus

A Wonder, returning back to me, you looked me straight in the eye
I realized who had been saved; it was not us, but rather the bee from I!
That was the moment my world turned on end
There was much more to know; my perception of life began to bend

Our relationship changed, and you took the wheel
I began to see there was so much to heal
With your faith in me, I was supported and grew
Into the partner that you always knew

We've worked with hundreds of humans, without judgment or white glove
Teaching connection, authenticity, and the power of unconditional love
You saw inside each one, without verdict or shame
With stories that were stuck, with your patience; they overcame

You showed me the endless wonder in this world
Sensing you now, your radiant light, something wants to arise from its swirl
Miracles are science we don't yet know, not some magical spell
To thrive in the world, we must live in the truth; to keep our hearts well

Goodbye, my good wizard; you taught me to see
All life on this planet is sacred, even that bee!
I'll know you again; I have faith in that spell
I sense you've found me already, but how I can't yet tell

You were a Warrior, a Wizard, a Wonder this I gladly accept
On the day the world lost you, countless connected hearts wept
Unconditional love was your magic, your gift to us all
You are still my beloved companion; you've answered my Soul's call

Resilience

Bounce back
Refuse to be succumbed by lack
Someone has your back
In a world about to crack

Outside it may be falling apart
Gasp, cry - but take heart
Inside is where to start
Nurture yourself; heal your heart

Light within shines
Flows through, you are one of a kind
Safe inside grows what's mine
Others want to crush, never you mind

Spring forth
Do not look back, only north
Love comes from a never ending source
Resilient, strong, stay the course

Resilient, unstoppable
Accomplished the improbable
Aligned with me, you are unstoppable
Believe and nothing is impossible.

Mission Possible

The wind has come up, the sea is alive
Out of the doldrums, it's time to high five!
Graces were received in the quiet and calm
The sun is rising, shedding light on a new dawn

During stillness and contemplation
Sufferings transformed into redemption
Old bones of stories gone dumped from the old pot
Each moment arrives empty, ready and waiting for what is or is not

You're a special agent in training
Open the briefcase; your mission; there'll be no complaining
Be the hands and feet of the collective of Souls
Partner, you've unveiled your greatness and broke your old mold

By your service, you reconnect, to all that you are
We have your back, there is nothing to fear
It is about unbecoming you see
To remember, remember who you were born to be

Journey of a Soul Family

Eight beings were all conceived in kind
All eight shared likeness in body and mind
Raised and nurtured together as one
Prepared by their parents for what was to come.

The children were loved and mostly played well together
However, their individualization seemed to take forever
Each entered their teens with an aim and a willful intent to be seen Eventually, each child turned eighteen, moved away; what does it all mean?

Their parental directives simple: Do What is Right and Just Be the Best. This advice was the catalyst they needed to be like none of the rest.
This little direction allowed them freedom and scope
Child by child, both parents prayed in patience and hope.

Society and culture influence life choices
How do we quiet these annoying, persuasive, loud voices?
Manmade distractions can turn down the volume
Eventually, that can lead to a life both stagnant and solemn.

Born with equal amounts of life force and potential
They made choices by following their heart and credential
The siblings in the beginning as all are now one
Living as witness to each other, have eight journeys done.

The mother and father, watching from heaven above
Look upon their soul child with the utmost of love
When the time comes again to gather together
The next journey begins for these birds of a feather.

White Bones

I am the bones of my ancestors
They define my strengths, fears, and character
Beneath my skin and muscle, my bones are white
Every creature with bones starts with the same right

What our Mother built upon these bones is a divine creation
Everything: a horse, a bird, a whale, a human - each one her pure ambition
No species, including humans, deserves more than another
Earth's diversity is passed through the bones of our great Mother

Secrets and memories are stored in the bones of old
Passed from generation to generation, survival is in the genetic code
Responsibility is given to each species to pass on good genes
Suffering transformed to wisdom keeps the genes clean

This is where humans lack and are stuck
Causing suffering across species, across generations, many don't give a cluck
Killing our own kind, killing for fun
Our Mother cries out, "What the cluck have I done?!"

When our suffering becomes a grudge It gets stuck deep in our bones and becomes foul genetic sludge
Our potential, mutated by fear and ethnic oppression
It's time to clean our genes - admit our faults, apologize, and question

Choose to transform, stop the ongoing sinning
With clean bones, you can remember who you were at the beginning
Remember that we all share one Mother – everything is connected
No matter what kind, color, shape or size – all life forms deserve to be respected

Warning: Colony Collapse

I gave you life, born as part of me, and my Earth
Six million years in gestation, then I gave birth
Humans, an unraveled thread from my fabric
You are my wild child, a rebellious maverick

But this is not about you, it is about the rest of us
We miss you; come back, return to my bust
Created in endless shapes and colors, my masterpiece
Remember that we are all one, to master peace

Warning signs come from many collaborative species
My honey bees, offered to take a loss for the human species
Take heed of their suffering; notice omens in their sacrifice
No, all of your science and theories shall not suffice

The bee colonies, parallel the collapse of you
See each other unconditionally; it is so simple to do
Your primal family pleads, restore your specie's closeness
Your survival hinges on unconditional love and wholeness

Honoring My Twin

Sometimes it seemed I've walked alone
But somehow felt like I was accompanied by a clone
But it is not my clone
It is my spiritual twin, I was never alone
He walked with me
And saw what I couldn't see
He cleared the path
And handled the wrath
He walked behind me
Protected me, so I could Be
He closed the loop behind
And taught me to be kind
Now I see him everywhere I look
He is my muse, the inspiration for my book.

Remembering Beauty

Snow, falling grace from heaven above
Buffers me from all that I still love
Sun rises in silence, the world has stood still
Out my window a black and white scene, no color, no frills

Outside surprised horses snort and paw in wonder
What is this place that offers a soft, white bed to slumber?
Layers, feathers of white, fall on their dense coat
My white mare looks at me intensely; demanding, I must take note

What is happening to me, to the land where I live?
I feel changes coming from above and below; what makes you think I am ready to give?
Shifting inside, love waits to flow through, to be received
Can it be true? To be worthy of this love, I find it hard to believe

This grand, white mare is quite something to behold
Arrived damaged and broken, transformation is beginning to unfold
On the outside, she is white, on the inside becoming black
Black Beauty, that is, confidence and strength, have found their way back

Once from a world brightly colored to old land stripped down to bare bones
Through grief and relief, I remember my Beauty; I am never alone
Omens and signs and everyday magic have summoned me here
Spring colors will come, ending this mournful year, for which I've shed my last tear

Seasons are cycles, the rhythm of nature
My next cycle in gestation, developing me for my future
What's ahead for me now grows from a love deep inside me, yet just out of sight
While I wait, I am nurtured by remembering and honoring my mares black and white

Serendipity is laying out the new path
With four-leaf clovers, lucky charms, at times illogical, not math
It's simple just ask, listen to what wants to be heard
Composing the messages, symbols, and rhymes into
Soul songs that won't go unheard.

The Dual Pilgrimage – Ode to Juano

A horse was born on the northern plains
He grew and served, as he was told, did not complain
A man was born in the northern plains
He grew and explored, courageously survived the heavy rains

His relationship with the humans served to self-serve
He was hardened by those that treated him in ways he did not deserve
His relationship with animals was to be sure that they served
He learned to produce, process and use animals; however, he did learn to conserve

It was his Soul's mission to connect with the human race
He found a fun way to do so; it was all about the horse race
It was his Soul's mission to connect with animals, to see them face to face
He found a fun way to do so, in the rainforest, learned at his own pace

Day by day, year by year, the stallion valiantly did what they asked
There was no job too small or too big; ask him anything, he'd be up to the task
Day by day, year by year, the man valiantly did what was asked
There was no job too small or too big; ask him anything, he'd be up for the task

One day Stallion said, "Soul, have I completed my mission?"
Soul answered, "No, Stallion, your pilgrimage carries on; it is time for a transition."
One day Man said, "Soul, is this all that there is, only hard work and making decisions?"
Soul answered, "No, Man, your pilgrimage carries on; it is time for a transition."

For Stallion, it was a day like any other, but it was not
A strange lady took him away, he had no idea he could be bought
For Man, it was a day like any other, but it was not
He rode up the hill to meet a lady stranger; what happened cannot be bought

The ideas about horses at the new place were strange
The stallion resisted, held firm to his idea of humans; it felt scary to change
The ideas about horses at this new place were strange
The man resisted, held firm to his idea of horses; it seemed scary to change

The strange humans held firm, with kindness and knowing
Played silly games, little by little, a new way to be began flowing
The strange humans held firm; eventually, their new way began showing
That horses are sentient beings, with loving hearts, relationships began growing

Stallion realized that humans, too, were sentient beings
"Soul, I can teach them to remember who they are." said Stallion, now seeing.
Man opened his heart to love, to trust, and to his own feelings
"Soul, Stallion taught me to remember who I am; I honor his life; he is a sentient being."

The mission for Stallion was now complete
"Man, I am proud to have grown with you; there is no longer a need to compete."
Man's mission carries on, there are new beings to meet
"Stallion, I am proud to have grown with you; you have taught me how it feels to be complete."

My Steve

A man that stands for everything that's right
Nothing can steer him away from this light
Contemplative, thoughtful and kind
When there are too many choices, he can't make up his mind

The home he creates is cozy and safe
You'll sleep well knowing he is your home base
If you are lucky, just maybe
He'll make you some chicken and gravy!

You'll never know anyone more loyal and true
He is undeniably devoted, one of a few
Backwards, forwards, this way and that
Only thing that could bother him is a gigantic, fat rat

Curious, brave, calm in a crisis
Frugal, conservative he'll find the best prices
Throw him a problem, none are too big
Give him a challenge, he'll tackle any gig

Songs in his head, start off his day
He takes everything in stride, what else can I say....
Oh yes, most important of all
He is my soulmate; he is my All

Up Rise or Rise Up?

Up Rise creates the impervious
Rise Up to be of service

Up Rise solidifies the mistaken
Rise Up to awaken

Up Rise breaks apart what wants to come next
Rise Up to see what's next, to connect

Up Rise crushes from the outside in
Rise Up, light up - from the inside out

Up Rise is asking to be saved
Rise Up, trust and be brave

The Great Turning Over

Time for the great turning over
Leave behind powering-over
Turn forward to power-with
See what in the past, was only myth

Oceans and seas are over suffering our plight
Water rising up, turning with powerful might
Forested mountains awaken from hiding
Diverse lands now prevail, run by nature residing

Those waiting for what is meant to unfold
Others backed by anger, attempt to control
In patient limbo, developing events still unknown
Desperately believing false facts on their phones

What divides conquers, a species in turmoil
It's time to choose. This is for real.
Open all three eyes, it's the new way of seeing
Get ready for a new greatness of being

Pollinators

Bee, sense the plants calling
Scout the location quickly, no stalling
Fly back to the hive
Communicate to the others, dance out the vibe

Off many workers go
Plants and flowers thankful to grow
The bees reap the benefit too
Life-sustaining, sweet honey, the glue

Human, sense Earth's calling
Use your intuition; with that, there is no falling
Retreat with kindred spirits
Sense the collective, feel us, to understand it

Be aware of the collapse of the hive
It's an indication of a deep dive
The midnight hour approaches
Stay true, authentic, and benevolent coaches

Off you must go now
Receptive ears are waiting to know
Benefits await; growth will be exponential
Connected to the whole in unlimited potential

Hot Air Balloon

Night air blankets the day
All that's been said has had its say
Under the covers, slowing heart rate
Lids close, the balloon inflates

Above the drama
Earth's never-ending diorama
Floating freely
Perspectives from here seen keenly

Leaving fright below
Time begins to slow
Directed by the divine
Knowing all will be fine

Below a low vibe
Pulling down to that side
Righteous turned wrong
Peace was here all along

But I have feet
Flying only a temporary retreat
Moments of fleeting peace
Allowing time for release

I'll stay here for now
Basket, balloon in the clouds
This high vibe divide
Observing it, not to hide

Landing with wings
Protective energy rings
Now strengthened, connected
Loved from above, always protected

Re-Wilding

The light of your roots
Dimmed by mean, crushing boots
Bound by what was unnatural
By items thought to be logical, practical

Who is the man, and who is the beast?
Is it not about claiming the win or defeat
What separates the two?
Find the line that divides; only one has a clue

To survive, you had to yield
The only choice, your fate was sealed
Fools could not see your spirit
Ears do not hear, see or believe in it

Your sacrifice under those boots
It's over, run wild, heal your roots
In this body, start over
Graze freely in fields of clover

Re-wild with the others
Your kin, your brothers
They nurture you as a colt
Free to kick and buck, lightning bolt!

When you find it's time
I will be here for you to find
My dear pony, not all humans are evil
We can have a cross-species love that is real

An Ode to Wild Souls

This is an ode to my soul
This is an ode to many souls
This is an ode to all souls
I am one part of the whole

Oh, kindred soul by my side
I've been left behind, unable to ride
Oh, kindred soul at my side
Walk with me, I have forgotten, be my guide

We walk, my soul with your soul
The forest opens to a vast, grassy knoll
Tiny flowers dot this meadow, breezes gently flow
My eyes, your eyes, many eyes see underneath the sun a glow

This is an ode to your soul
This is an ode to many souls
This is an ode to all souls
You are one part of the whole

We stop, two souls at peace, at rest
Above the meadow, an eagle brings food back to the nest
Mountains tower over us, no need to climb their snowy crest
Here all creatures, all souls are connected with the rest.

Our souls are found at last
The ground vibrates; a rising energy comes thundering past
We rise up too, our souls are called to join the wild rest
We are part of the wild whole, remembering, we become one with the rest

This is an ode to any wild soul
This is an ode to all wild souls
This is an ode to every wild soul
We are all one part of the wild whole

Pillars of Grief

Its thick, dark shell separates the dead from the living: Grief
Hiding within, day in and day out, a confusing and clever energy thief
An impenetrable canopy, held up by uncomfortable feelings
Pillars of emotion must fall, to begin the healing

Sometimes things are not as they seem; people in places they don't belong
Disappointment: a failed capacity to see others true intention all along
Faith in design, in plan and focus, ulterior motives in a false team
Pillar *Betrayal* creeps into the shadows, strengthens by not being seen

Anger pushes up from inside; who is this, that takes what is mine?
Setting boundaries can create selfish monsters, and monsters aren't kind.
Monsters take and take until they've had their fill, then move on to their next kill
Worthlessness is what remains after the take, stripped of ideas, inventive frill

When all is gone, with no more to take, it is goodbye
The pillars of *Loneliness, Abandonment,* and *Anxiety* join, with no alibi
Depression supports the canopy of grief, fortifying the emotional muddle
Soul cries out, "Stop the madness before all that remains is a puddle!"

Fear and *Vulnerability* enjoy a daily dance: "Will we die of this disease; what lies ahead?"
The emotional pillars intensify, demanding attention, "Take the lead, do not be led."
One by one, acknowledged, processed, then thanked for their role
Grief turns into wisdom, pillars crumble, the canopy falls, thus saving this sad soul.

Mime To Have Some Fun

Pandas carrying umbrellas
Mimes are such funny fellas
Bears in yoga poses
In a hammock a Mime doses

Bees in yellow jackets
The Mime ignores the racket
Raccoons hum a mellow tune
While the Mime contemplates the moon

Lighting bugs hold tiny lanterns
The Mime swirls, making the rings 'round Saturn
Chihuahuas wearing tiny sweaters
It begins to rain; the Mime gets wetter and wetter

Bats in boots
An owl screeches, "What a hoot!"
The Mime, still mute
Begins to play his flute

A big red horse gives a speech
A black cat and woodchuck agree to meet
"Shush," says the Mime, rising to his feet"
"It's time for me too to speak!"

Mime time has begun
He is ready to have some fun!
The audience has gathered round
Silently waiting for the Mime's sound!

The Choice

To know shame
Is part of a complex game
Entwined with guilt, lacks cover
When unraveled, transforms into honor

Now to choose
Choose shame and cower
Choose honor and recover
Loose or win, you choose

Experiencing abandonment
Is part of the game plan
To leave or be left, who ran?
Either way, it is to know commitment

Now to choose
Choose to be alone
Choose commitment and be grown
Stay small or grow, it's your choice

Betrayal is a grave sin
A seemingly an impossible win
A high stakes move that destroys solidarity
To know it is to know true love and loyalty

Now to choose
Choose to be broken
Choose to be awoken
Shrivel or rise, you choose

Passings

Callings become the fuel of stagnation
It's a gift to be called, a late realization
The lowly struggle to quantify brilliance
Only one factor counts, its resilience

In deep sleep, I sense my resistance
Its strength blinds me, binds me, it's persistent
What is calling me? Who is behind these forces?
When I yield and listen, I am offered the right resources

Opening to the flow, I become a conduit of light
Energy passes through me, now things feel right
The callings pass through me, flow from me, supporting
Conducting for those asking, I serve to connect by connecting

Becoming an ambassador for the whole
Open to love all beings, all creatures, all souls
Allowing the enlightened connection to pass through
Helps heal the Earth, restoring her vitality, as it heals me too

Trinity

Majestic tree tall and grand
Roots planted firmly in the land
Your reflection in the stillness of the pond
A shimmering testament, you are where you belong

Opposite the mirror of your reflection
Lies a stark contrast asking for introspection
You cast darkness in the meadow
Morning frost survives in your shadow

Oh, grand one, standing right in the middle
In still waters, your reflection is part of this riddle
Your shadow holds something to be discovered
Sun lights the shadow, and the mystery is uncovered

We are a symbiotic trinity, three dimensions
Our being, our shadows, our reflection
We are, we learn, we project
These self-truths we must respect

Faith in Unfurling

What is this pressure that I feel?
I have been sleeping and floating for so long; is it real?
My quiet cocoon is not so soft anymore
Now I am sensing increasing pressure right to my core

There is pressure around me, pushing me in
I am getting uncomfortable; what is clamping onto my skin?
The pressure against me pushes me to go
I feel like a transmitter of this energy; it's asking me to grow

Here it comes the pressure again, pushing and pushing
My water is leaking away from me; now not leaking, but gushing
Something inside me wants to stretch and uncurl
I begin to yearn for something, my body starts to unfurl

In the birth process, we did suffer
This is something I know, as does every mother
Once born, the suffering is transformed
Changed into love, energizing the lifelong bond that has formed

Glance behind, look ahead
Now grateful not to be dead
Life's problems tightly curled
With faith it will unfurl

Soul Parenting

Today you start your journey
Grow, learn, explore, create; there is no hurry
I'll care for you with mine and all of our hearts
Always we are one, our hearts are never meant to part

You'll spend some earth years learning about the world
Setting goals, celebrating achievements, as your skills unfurl
In time, the preparatory journey to maturity comes to an end
When you are ready, things shift, and the pilgrimage begins, my friend

Trust me enough to be brave
Of course, there'll be times you won't behave!
You are first, a human be one; remember to have fun
We have fun too, pay attention to the signs, we are playsome

An unfolding event will lead you to your path
Pay attention to the omens, caterpillar in the grass
Remembering who you were born to be
You are a butterfly; this is the real adventure you'll see!

Along the way, actions taken are to serve the collective
Plan your accomplishments to support this prime directive
Ask us for what you need on this earthly quest
There is support along the way; things to manifest

Alone you are not; you are one part of the whole
You have a choice, so choose a contribution that raises up all souls
Your pilgrimage unveils your responsibility
Remembering who you were born to be, is the key to your tranquility

Game On

Time move up, join the rest
Get ready to play some chess
You needed this period to rest
After all, you'd been put to the test

Time to stand in your glory
Proud to tell all your story
Remember who was the author?
You'll reap the rewards, be open to offers

Time to enjoy this freedom
Founded on peace, a new kingdom
Time to believe you're no phony
Surrounded by horses, chickens, and Pony

Time to lift your heart high
Release the last doubt; look up to the sky
Wisdom replaced betrayal, grief, and anger
Always protected by us, you're not in danger

Time to stand firm in your calling
The cocoon has opened, no more stalling
The old kingdom is gone
Chess pieces thrown on the lawn

Time to let the game be reset
Keep the memories, lessons; don't forget
That old board belongs to others now
Every piece of the place right down to the cow

Time to learn some new moves
Game is in play, get into the groove
My dear, have no worries
You'll understand before the first flurry

Contemplations

www.ingramcontent.com/pod-product-compliance
Lightning Source LLC
Chambersburg PA
CBHW042002150426
43194CB00002B/99